WELCOME TO

GRAND CANYON

NATIONAL PARK

BY TERI AND BOB TEMPLE

Content Consultant: Libby Schaaf, Supervisory Park Ranger, Division of Interpretation, Grand Canyon National Park

MAP KEY

The maps throughout this
book use the following icons:

🚗 Driving Excursion

🥾 Hiking Trail

🏠 Lodging

⛺ Campground

🔭 Overlook

⛱ Picnic Area

✴ Point of Interest

🧍 Ranger Station

🐿 Squirrels

❓ Visitor Center

About National Parks

A national park is an area of land that has been set aside by Congress. National parks protect nature and history. In most cases, no hunting, grazing, or farming is allowed. The first national park in the United States—and in the world—was Yellowstone National Park. It is located in parts of Wyoming, Idaho, and Montana. It was founded in 1872. In 1916, the U.S. National Park Service began.

Today, the National Park Service manages more than 380 sites. Some of these sites are historic, such as the Statue of Liberty or Martin Luther King, Jr. National Historic Site. Other park areas preserve wild land. The National Park Service manages 40% of the nation's wilderness areas, including national parks. Each year, millions of people from around the world visit these national parks. Visitors may camp, go canoeing, or go for a hike. Or, they may simply sit and enjoy the scenery, wildlife, and the quiet of the land.

TABLE OF

The Child's World®

**Published in the
United States of America
by The Child's World®**

PO Box 326
Chanhassen, MN 55317-0326
800-599-READ
www.childsworld.com

Acknowledgements

The Child's World®: Mary Berendes, Publishing Director

The Design Lab: Kathleen Petelinsek, Design and Page Production

Map Hero, Inc.: Matt Kania, Cartographer

Red Line Editorial: Bob Temple, Editorial Direction

Photo Credits
Cover and this page: Ron Watts/Corbis.

Interior: BrandXPictures: 1, 2–3; Buddy Mays/Corbis:16; Corbis: 13; David Muench/Corbis: 6–7 (top), 12, 14, 15, 27; Galen Rowell/Corbis: 25; Gunter Marx Photography/Corbis: 22–23; James Sparshatt/Corbis: 10–11; Larry Lee Photography/Corbis: 8; Marc Muench/Corbis: 18–19; Nevin Kempthorne Fleet/David

**Library of Congress
Cataloging-in-Publication Data**

Temple, Teri.
 Welcome to Grand Canyon National Park / by Teri Temple and Bob Temple.
  p. cm. — (Visitor guides)
 Includes index.
 ISBN 1-59296-697-7 (library bound : alk. paper)
 1. Grand Canyon National Park (Ariz.)—Juvenile literature. I. Temple, Bob. II. Title. III. Series.
 F788.T46 2006
 917.91'3202—dc22   2005030080

On the cover and this page
The view from the top of Toroweap Point provides one of the best views of the Grand Canyon. Toroweap (or Tuweep) Point is located on the canyon's North Rim.

On page 1
The Grand Canyon seems to be even more beautiful at sunrise.

On pages 2–3
It seems as if you can see for miles from the top of Grandview Point, the highest point on the canyon's South Rim.

WELCOME TO GRAND CANYON NATIONAL PARK

∧

CONTENTS

Natural Wonder

Grand Canyon National Park

ARIZONA

Welcome to Grand Canyon National Park! The Grand Canyon is one of the most spectacular natural wonders of the world. Here, in the northwest corner of Arizona, you'll find a rocky wilderness that drops nearly a mile (1.6 km) down into the earth. Desert wildflowers and prickly cactus can be found in this rocky landscape.

An amazing collection of plants and animals can be seen here. Because of the different **elevations** in the park, a variety of **ecosystems** formed over time. Mule deer live on the canyon rim. They graze on the low sagebrush in the early morning. The canyon floor is more like a desert. The Colorado River runs through the canyon. It creates yet another habitat.

Be sure to pick up a nature pamphlet found along some of the trails. It will tell you all about the wildlife that makes its home in the park.

🚶🚶 Marble Canyon is the northernmost section of the Grand Canyon. Its narrow walls open up into the much wider canyon beyond.

Squirrel Cousins

Two of the park's smaller **inhabitants** are the Abert's and Kaibab squirrels. They both live in the Grand Canyon, but on opposite sides! As the canyon was created, the forests of the Abert's (left) and Kaibob (right) squirrels became separated. Kaibab squirrels can only be found in the Ponderosa Pines of the northern rim. Abert's squirrels live on the south side.

Glen Canyon Dam was built between 1956 and 1966. It stands 3,700 feet (1,128 m) high and is made of concrete. The waters behind the dam create Lake Powell, which took 17 years to completely fill after the dam was built.

Eroding Landscape

Look across the canyon. You'll notice the spectacular views and the canyon's large size. The colorful rock layers tell the canyon's story. Scientists can learn about our past from the **artifacts** and clues they find in them.

Where did this amazing canyon come from? How was it made?

The Colorado River has flowed across the land since before the canyon existed. Scientists believe that millions of years ago, the land on the Colorado **Plateau** began to shift and rise. The river remained. It cut its way through as the rocky land rose. This is one of the many theories of how the canyon was made. We do know this change came slowly. The top layers of the land were made of sedimentary rock. This kind of rock erodes, or wears away, easily. The river didn't have to work very hard to carve its path.

Today the river runs through a layer of rock made up of schist and granite. Since these kinds of rocks are much harder, the river causes very little erosion each year. Glen Canyon dam helps prevent erosion. The Grand Canyon you see today is the result of millions of years of erosion.

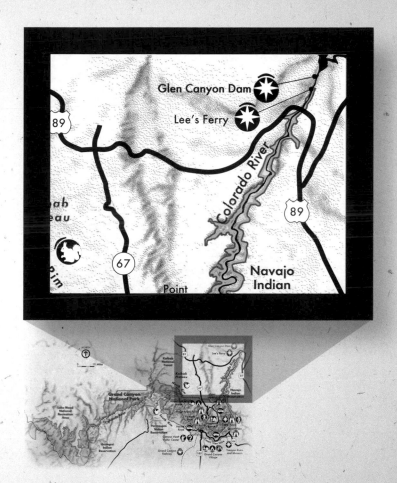

Life Zones, Top to Bottom

From the top of the canyon rim to its desert-like floor, the weather is unpredictable. The climate changes with the season.

Spring arrives late, but brings with it colorful wildflowers. Look for bighorn sheep as they move easily among the rocks. Make time to join a park ranger for a nature walk or an evening star watch.

Summers at the rim can be warm but pleasant. Be ready for thunderstorms, though. They can arrive unexpectedly. Thunderstorms usually bring lightning, which makes it very dangerous to be near the canyon rim during storms. If you hike into the canyon in the summer, be prepared for a heat wave. The temperature will be much warmer on the canyon floor!

Lightning lights up the sky over the Grand Canyon during a thunderstorm. Lightning is a stream of electricity that super-heats the air around it. Just one flash (lasting only half of one second) heats the surrounding air to a temperature that's five times hotter than the surface of the sun—that's about 50,000 F (27,760 C)!

Lee's Ferry is thought of as the beginning of the Grand Canyon. All of the mile markers throughout the park are based on their distance from the Ferry. The area is named for John D. Lee, who moved to the area in 1871 and created a ferry (a boat crossing) to help people cross the Colorado River. The ferry was used until 1928, when a bridge was finally built over Marble Canyon.

The fall brings cooler temperatures. It is also the best time for fishing in the Colorado River. Fishing is easy at Lee's Ferry, but difficult elsewhere in Grand Canyon. Look high on the mountainside. You'll see Gambel oak exploding with fall color. Winter is just around the corner.

California Condor

One of the rarest birds found in the Grand Canyon is the California condor. It is the largest land bird in North America. Its wingspan is nearly 10 feet (3 m). This magnificent bird almost became **extinct**. Today the California condor is slowly recovering in the wild. Look for the California condor as it soars above the canyon.

Snow covers trees on the South Rim. Winter weather in the Grand Canyon can change quickly, and roads and trails can become icy and dangerous. The main road to the North Rim closes completely from November to May due to heavy snowfall.

The silence is what you'll remember about a winter canyon visit. The muted layers of rock look like another world after a snowfall. Winter can also bring freezing temperatures and snowstorms. Watch out for ice as you hike along the snow-covered trails. No matter when you visit, there are endless things to do and see!

Ancient Indian Culture

The Ancestral Puebloans were part of an ancient desert Native American culture. They lived in the Grand Canyon about 1,500 years ago. They lived in adobe buildings called pueblos. The Ancestral Puebloans are the **ancestors** of the present-day Hopi people. You can learn about their culture at the Tusayan Ruins and Museum.

The Nankoweap ruins are high above a valley in the North Rim area. The ruins were once an ancient granary where Ancentral Puebloans stored squash and corn. They chose the site because it was difficult to get to, therefore their food was kept safe from mice and thieves.

Path to Tourism

Humans have lived in and around the canyon for more than 10,000 years. The first inhabitants were Native Americans, and some still live in the canyon today. From the ancient Ancestral Puebloans to the Navajos, Native Americans have helped shape the land.

In the late 1800s the U.S. tried to promote the Grand Canyon as an area rich in natural resources. Many miners came to stake their claims. They found plenty of copper, zinc, and lead. Their problem was getting the materials out of the canyon, which took a lot of money and time.

Spanish Explorers

In 1540, a Spanish explorer named Coronado set off on an expedition from Mexico into the U.S. Southwest. The group was in search of the legendary "Seven Cities of Gold." Instead, they found the Grand Canyon, with the help of Hopi guides. The explorers soon left, however. They were frustrated by the enormous canyon.

Numerous narrow canyons run through Grand Canyon National Park. They often carry water fed by underground springs through narrow passages and pools inhabited by fish and frogs.

Many people thought the canyon would be a beautiful place for people to visit. Photographers, writers, and artists helped spread the word. They produced beautiful works of art that showed the natural wonders of the canyon. Soon visitors wanted to see the Grand Canyon for themselves.

President Woodrow Wilson wanted to protect this special place. In 1919, the Grand Canyon became a national park in order to preserve this land forever.

The Powell Expedition

Major John Powell was the first man to lead an expedition along the Colorado River through the Grand Canyon, in 1869. A one-armed Civil War veteran, he braved rapids, heat, and the loss of three men on his journey. His notes provided a great deal of information about the area.

Exploring the Grand Canyon

G rand Canyon National Park has three distinct areas. Each area would take several days to explore. Even though it is a very large place, you can still see a lot of the park in just one day.

The South Rim draws the most visitors. It has spectacular views. Here, trees like the piñon pine and Utah juniper have learned to live with little water. They have adapted to the hot, dry climate. Be on the lookout for the acrobatic flights of ravens soaring along the cliffs.

Arrive at the park in style aboard the Grand Canyon Railway. Then begin your day at the Canyon View Visitor Center. Here you'll find everything you'll need to have a successful day in the park. From the visitor center, you can head to the east or to the west and start exploring.

The Grand Canyon Railway is a great way to learn more about the canyon and the areas around it. The railway began in 1901, and its engines have been restored to look the way they did 100 years ago. Trips on the railway run between the town of Williams, Arizona and Grand Canyon Village.

The Kolb Studio was the home and studio of Emery and Ellsworth Kolb, two brothers who came to the Grand Canyon in the early 1900s. The Kolbs became known for their photography and filmmaking, and were the first to film a boat trip down the Colorado River with a movie camera.

If you head east, you'll travel along Desert View Drive. Stop at the many scenic overlooks. Then travel back in time as you walk thorough the ruins of an ancient pueblo at the Tusayan Ruins and Museum.

If you decide to go west, you will find yourself heading toward Grand Canyon Village and Hermit's Road. Stop at the Yavapai Observation Station and see a panoramic view of the canyon from its windows. Be sure to check out the art gallery at Kolb Studio. Don't miss Verkamp's Curios, one of the canyon's oldest stores!

Into the Canyon

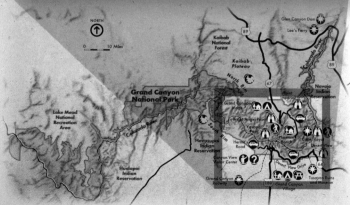

There are only a few ways into the canyon to explore the rich life on its floor. You can walk, or you can ride a mule down the trails. You can also ride the rapids of the Colorado River on a river raft. Any way you choose to arrive, it will be a journey you will never forget.

The Grand Canyon is 277 miles (446 km) long, 18 miles (29 km) at its widest point, and reaches more than a mile (1.6 km) deep. The floor of the canyon is hot and dry, except along the riverbed. It is home to a very different collection of plants and animals. Here you find giant lizards like the chuckwalla. The **nocturnal** ring-tailed cat also makes its home here. Cactus and desert wildflowers also grow here.

Travelers who brave the trails to the bottom should plan to spend the night. It is extremely difficult to go to the bottom of the canyon and back to the top in one day. For the overnight visitors, there are Phantom Ranch cabins and Bright Angel Campground. As night comes, stare up at the endless stars. Let the sound of the river lull you to sleep.

Seeing the canyon by taking a "mule train" is a popular activity. These slow-paced trips are sometimes the only way for people to see hard-to-reach areas of the park. The mules are very surefooted, which is a good thing—sometimes the paths are just wide enough for the mules, with a steep drop just inches away from their hooves!

North Rim – the Quiet Gem

Our last area to explore is the more **isolated** North Rim. The North Rim is often called the "other" Grand Canyon. It is its own unique world. It features a different climate, scenery, and wildlife. Because it is so isolated, it is still very wild, but peaceful.

It rains and snows more on the north side. The plants and animals here have adapted to a wetter climate. Large pines like the ponderosa pine and Douglas fir tower overhead. The large fields of grass are perfect for grazing wildlife.

Take a self-guided nature tour out to Cape Royal. Along the way you can see Angel's Window, a natural arch in the rocks. More adventurous travelers can hike down to the Coconino Overlook or the Supai Tunnel. Both offer wonderful views into the canyon. The best view of the canyon, however, is at Point Imperial. It provides an amazing view of the canyon and the surrounding area from the highest point on either rim.

The Grand Canyon is a wide, deep canyon carved over time. It is a gift from past generations.

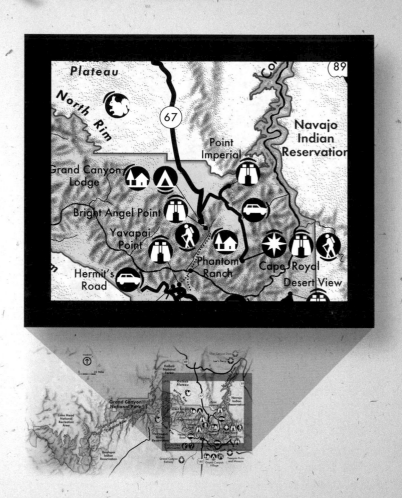

It reminds us to appreciate the beauty of the world around us. Come and discover the wonders of this amazing place.

🚶🚶 Sunrise over the canyon's North Rim area is a beautiful sight. Watching the sun rise is a very popular activity in the park. Views are greatly affected by air quality, and air is usually clearer during the winter months.

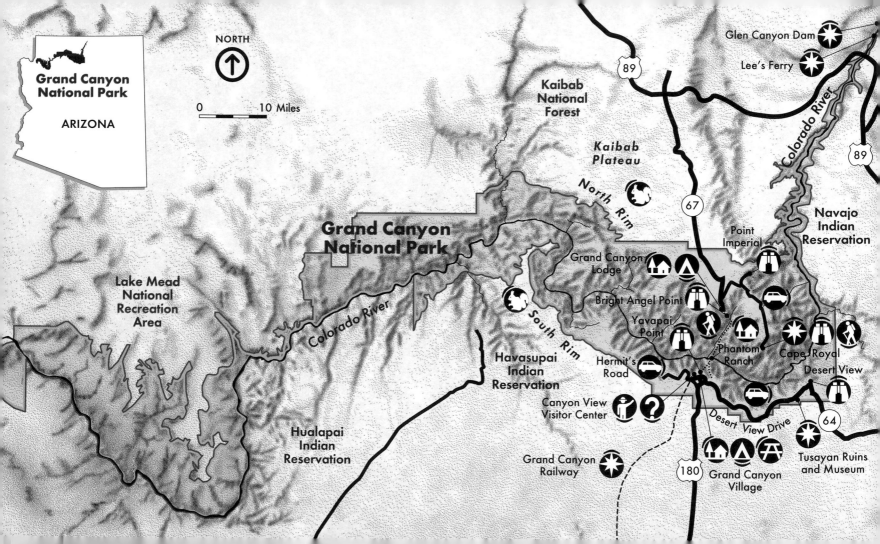

Grand Canyon National Park

ARIZONA

NORTH

0   10 Miles

Glen Canyon Dam

Lee's Ferry

89

Colorado River

89

Kaibab
National
Forest

Kaibab
Plateau

North Rim

67

Navajo
Indian
Reservation

Point
Imperial

Grand Canyon
National Park

Grand Canyon
Lodge

Bright Angel Point

Yavapai
Point

Phantom
Ranch

Cape Royal

Desert View

Lake Mead
National
Recreation
Area

Colorado River

South Rim

Havasupai
Indian
Reservation

Hermit's
Road

Canyon View
Visitor Center

Desert View Drive

64

Hualapai
Indian
Reservation

Grand Canyon
Railway

180

Grand Canyon
Village

Tusayan Ruins
and Museum

GRAND CANYON NATIONAL PARK FAST FACTS

Date founded: February 26, 1919

Location: Northwest corner of Arizona

Size: 1,904 square miles/4,931 sq km; 1,218,560 acres/ 493,134 hectares

Major habitats: Mountain, desert, streamside (also called riparian)

Important landforms: Canyon, plateaus, basins, rock formations, rock layers of previous time periods, fossils

Elevation:
  Highest: 8,803 feet/2.68 km (Point Imperial, North Rim)
  Lowest: 2,480 feet/0.76 km (Canyon Bottom)

Weather:
  Average yearly rainfall: 26 inches/66 cm at rim; 9 inches/23 cm at floor
  Average temperatures: 62 F/17 C to 30 F/-1 C at rim; 82 F/28 C to 56 F/13 C at floor
  Highest temperature: 91 F/33 C (1989)
  Lowest temperature: –24 F/-31 C (1985)

Number of animal species: 91 mammal species, 56 kinds of reptiles and amphibians, 17 species of fish, and more than 373 kinds of birds

Main animal species: Bobcats, coyotes, mule deer, squirrels, desert bighorn sheep, rattlesnakes, red-tailed hawks, golden eagles, piñon jays, and California condors

Number of plant species: More than 1,500

Main plant species: Ponderosa pine, piñon pine, cliffrose, fernbush, serviceberry, prickly pear cactus, asters, Indian paintbrushes, yucca plant, cacti, and willow

Number of endangered or threatened animal/plant species: 8—Humpback chub, Kanab ambersnail, Mexican spotted owl, razorback sucker, peregrine falcon, Southwestern willow flycatcher, California condor, and sentry milk vetch

Native people: Pueblo, Hopi, Havasupai, Hualapai, Navajo, Paiute, Zuni

Number of visitors each year: About 4.5 million

Important sites and landmarks: East and West rim drives, Yavapai Observation Station, Desert View Watchtower, Tusayan Ruins and Museum, Kolb Studio, Grand Canyon Lodge, Coconino Overlook and Supai Tunnel, Point Imperial, Bright Angel Point, and Angels Window Overlook

Tourist activities: Ranger-led walks and talks, hiking, backpacking, camping, fishing, river rafting, mule and horseback trail rides, riding Grand Canyon Railway, aerial tours

GLOSSARY

ancestors (AN-ses-turz): Your ancestors are members of your group or family that lived a long time ago. The Ancestral Puebloans are the ancestors of the Hopi people of today.

artifacts (ART-ih-fakts): Artifacts are objects made or changed by human beings. Scientists have found many artifacts in Grand Canyon National Park.

ecosystems (EE-koh-sis-tumz): Ecosystems are communities of plants and animals interacting with their environment. There are seven different ecosystems found at the Grand Canyon.

elevations (el-leh-VAY-shunz): Elevation is the height of land above sea level. The highest elevation at the Grand Canyon is at Point Imperial.

extinct (ek-STINGKT): If a type of plant or animal is extinct, it has died out forever. Many of the native Colorado River fish are in danger of becoming extinct because of the dams. Some species have already become extinct.

inhabitants (in-HAB-ih-tunts): The people or creatures who live in a certain place are its inhabitants. The Kaibab squirrel is an inhabitant of the North Rim.

isolated (EYE-soh-lay-ted): When something is separate, or not very close to anything else, it is isolated. The North Rim is isolated because it is difficult to reach.

nocturnal (nok-TURN-ull): A nocturnal animal is active at night. The nocturnal ring-tailed cat comes out at night to feed on insects and berries.

plateau (pla-TOH): A plateau is an area of high, flat land. The Grand Canyon was once a plateau.

TO FIND OUT MORE

FURTHER READING

Hall, Margaret.
Grand Canyon National Park.
Chicago: Heinemann Library, 2006.

Justesen, Jim Williams and Judy Newhouse (illustrator).
"Hey Ranger!" Kids Ask Questions about Grand Canyon National Park.
Guilford, CT.: Falcon, 2006.

Lomberg, Michelle.
Grand Canyon: The Largest Canyon in the United States.
New York: Weigl Publishers, 2004.

ON THE WEB

Visit our home page for lots of links
about Grand Canyon National Park:

http://www.childsworld.com/links

NOTE TO PARENTS, TEACHERS, AND LIBRARIANS:
We routinely check our Web links to make sure
they're safe, active sites—so encourage your
readers to check them out!